STANDARD PROGRAM BOOK

for Easter

Includes materials for
Mother's Day and Father's Day

compiled by

Pat Fittro

STANDARD PUBLISHING
Cincinnati, Ohio

Scripture taken from the HOLY BIBLE, NEW INTERNATIONAL VERSION®. NIV®. Copyright © 1973, 1978, 1984 by International Bible Society. Used by permission of Zondervan Publishing House. All rights reserved.

The Standard Publishing Company, Cincinnati, Ohio
A division of Standex International Corporation
©1996 by The Standard Publishing Company
All rights reserved
Printed in the United States of America

ISBN 0-7847-0467-8

Contents

Easter

Recitations

Easy	5
Medium	8
Difficult	13

Exercises 22

Programs 28

Mother's Day 34

Father's Day 42

A Place Prepared

Helen Kitchell Evans

The lovely white Easter lily
  Makes us think of God's glory
For it reminds each of us
  Of the marvelous Easter story.

How Jesus was placed in the tomb,
  How He arose in victory,
And lives with the heavenly Father
  In a place prepared for you and
    me.

Have a Blessed Easter

Easy

An Easter Welcome

Lucy Robbins

We welcome you this Easter Day.
Come right in without delay.
We are here to sing and say,
"Christ the Lord is risen today!"

Glad You Came

Iris Gray Dowling

We are so glad you came today,
We really hope you'll want to stay,
We have so much for you to hear—
An Easter message full of hope
  and cheer.

Easter

Saundra Birmingham

Easter brings
Blessed things!

Welcome Guest

Helen Kitchell Evans

I may be small and very young
  And sometimes I'm a pest,
But I'm here this morning
  To say, "Each one here is a
    welcome guest."

Easter Children

Saundra Birmingham

Yes Ma'am, Yes Sir
Little children love Easter!

A Happy Day

Cora M. Owen

Oh, what a happy, happy day!
Let all the earth rejoice!
For Christ arose! He'll never die!
I praise with heart and voice.

Good Morning

Helen Kitchell Evans

Good morning, everyone. *(Open
  arms to congregation.)*
So glad to see each of you here.
  (Point to various people.)
May you find a blessing,
May your hearts be filled with
  cheer.

He'll Come Back

Cora M. Owen

Jesus lives forever.
  He arose one day.
Now He lives in Heaven.
  He'll come back some day.

We Know

Carolyn R. Scheidies

Though we are young,
   This we know,
   Jesus came,
     Because He loves us so.

Welcome

Dixie Phillips

I'm ____ years old as you can see.
My parents are very proud of me!
Because I have come to welcome
   you *(Point.)*
And your video cameras too!

Very Small

Dixie Phillips

To you, *(Point.)* I might look very
   small.
And certainly, I'm not *(Shake
   head.)* very tall.
But I am big enough to say,
"Welcome to our Easter play!"

Looking for the Savior

Saundra Birmingham

I'm not looking for the bunny
I'm not looking for the egg;
I'm looking for the Savior
Whose precious blood was shed.

So Happy

Dixie Phillips

I'm so happy! I've just got to say,
"We're so glad you've come to our
   Easter play!"

Then and Now

Saundra Birmingham

He was the Savior then
Though men wouldn't believe
   Him;
He is the Savior now
And men still won't receive Him.

Love and Life

Saundra Birmingham

He gave His love
   That we might know,
A way of righteousness
   In a world of woe.

He gave His life
   That we might live,
Together with the Father
   And the blessings He gives.

Easter Love

Saundra Birmingham

No Easter egg,
No Easter toy,
Just Easter love
   For every girl and boy.

With Cheer

Helen Kitchell Evans

Happy Easter to each one
We're so glad you are here;
May Easter bring you happiness
And days filled with cheer.

The Lord Needs Me

Helen Kitchell Evans

I am very little
But still the Lord needs me,
So I'll help when I can
And do it happily.
Easter greetings to everyone!

Why He Rose

Dolores Steger

I know why my Lord rose;
It's quite plain to see;
He rose to take care of
And walk beside me!

An Easter Limerick

Iris Gray Dowling

Some people think that God is
    dead,
But I can tell you what I read:
He's alive in Heaven today;
I have faith in His way
And I believe what He said.

Showers of Blessings

Nell Ford Hann

The spring showers,
    Bring forth flowers,
        That is what's been told to me;

I am confessing,
    I've showers of blessings,
        Paid for me . . . . . at Calvary!

Easter Action Poem

Dixie Phillips

(Children line up in straight line in front of the church.)

The disciples did cry and cry!
(Rub eyes.)
For their friend, Jesus, did die.
(Hold arms out like a cross, then drop head down.)
But their tears turned to smiles
    that Easter Day. *(Rub eyes and then stop and cup hands around face and smile.)*
For Jesus had risen from the grave.
(Raise arms toward the ceiling.)

Farewell We Say

Helen Kitchell Evans

Farewell, farewell
    This happy Easter Day;
We have tried to make you happy
    So now farewell we say.
(To be used by 1 child or 3. Each speaks one line, all on last.)

Medium

We Welcome You

Saundra Birmingham

We welcome you this Easter
   To share this glorious day;
We offer you our risen Savior
   And the love He came to portray.

We invite your kind applause
   And your participation, too;
Most of all we take great delight
   In presenting our program to you.

Hallelujah, He Lives

Iris Gray Dowling

My heart is full of joy—
   That is why I want to sing;
This the day to celebrate
   The life of Jesus Christ, my King.

Rejoice!

Alta McLain

We can be very glad today
   For Jesus lives. He made a way
   To give us life forever more.
   With love He opened Heaven's door.
Rejoice! Oh give our Savior praise.
He paid the price and blessed our days.

Little Chick

Dolores Steger

Little chick, little chick,
Peeping from the shell,
Chirping out the story
That you have to tell,
How you were in darkness,
Waiting, patiently,
To come out, like Jesus,
Arising new and free.

New Life...
God's Special Blessing

Whenever I Think

Dixie Phillips

Whenever I think of spring,
I think of this one thing!
How Jesus left Heaven above,
And gave us His gift of love.
His own precious life, He gave,
But He didn't stay long in the grave.
He arose with life anew,
He arose for me and for you.
   (Point.)
He lives again,
In the hearts of men!

God Gave

Cora M. Owen

For God so loved the world
He gave His only Son.
One night in Bethlehem,
Giving of love was done.
For God so loved the world,
He gave His only son,
One day at Calvary,
The work of love was done.

The Story

Dolores Steger

The Bible tells the story
  That each one of us knows,
How Jesus died to save us
  And, then, on Easter, rose.

It's more than just a story
  Like others told to you;
I can tell, with all my heart,
  It's God's Word, and it's true!

Jesus Is Mine

Cora M. Owen

Jesus is mine!
  I'm glad He lives!
New life is mine,
  This life He gives.

Jesus is mine!
  He walks with me.
Because He lives,
  From sin, I'm free.

Let Him Know

Helen Kitchell Evans

You folks look extra joyful
  Could it be the day?
This glorious day called Easter
  When the stone was rolled away.
When Jesus brought salvation
  To all people everywhere.
Let's sing His praise this morning
  To let Him know we care.

(Follow with a song.)

I Love to Think of Easter

Cora M. Owen

I love to think of Easter,
  And how the Savior lives,
How He arose in victory,
  And how new life He gives.

I love to think of Easter,
  And how it brings us joy;
How we can have a gladness,
  That nothing can destroy.

Easter . . . Unchanged

Nell Ford Hann

Cars may be a little newer,
   A whole lot faster, too;
Hair and clothing styles may
   change,
   As well as fads, trends and
   attitudes.

The hymns offered in praise to
   God,
   On Easter Sunday morn,
Are as fresh and new to me today,
   As when my grandparents were
   born.

Unto Him

C. R. Scheidies

Recitation for one or two individuals or groups

Under the rays of the warm spring
   sun,
The last icicle crackles, breaks,
   plummets down,
Shattering the last chill image of
   winter,
On the newly awakened ground.

Like He who warms our hearts,
Breaks the hold of bondage and
   sin,
By His resurrection power,
And draws us unto Him.

Song: "To God Be the Glory"

He Is Not Dead

Wanda E. Brunstetter

Jesus died upon a cross,
To save the world from sin,
God suffered such an awful loss,
So we could be with Him.

But He did not stay dead,
Because in three days He rose,
He came back to life instead,
He is not dead as every Christian
   knows!

We Give Thanks

Helen Kitchell Evans

We give thanks this Easter
   That God sent Jesus from above,
We give thanks for His life
   And for His everlasting love.

We give thanks He brought
   salvation,
   We know He loves us dearly.
That's the reason we celebrate
   This special day yearly.

I'm Saved—I Live

Cora M. Owen

I'm saved because He died,
And shed His blood for me.
He took away my sin
On cross of Calvary.

I live because He lives.
He rose to justify.
He gave eternal life,
I'll never never die.

From Above

Helen Kitchell Evans

It must have been wonderful
  To have seen the stone rolled
    away,
To have seen only an empty tomb
  Where the body of Jesus lay.

How wonderful to know
  Jesus now gives His love
To all the Christian people
  From His home in Heaven above.

Rolled Away

Kay Hoffman

Lord, send the angel like you did
  That first glad Easter day
That from our rock-sealed hearts
  The stone be rolled away.

The stone of cold indifference
  To the spiritual need
That keeps man's heart entombed
  In selfishness and greed.

On this another Easter Day
  May the stone be rolled away
That the risen Christ would come
  Into each heart to stay.

Why Jesus Died

Alyce Pickett

Jesus died for you and me,
Because He wanted us to be
With Him in Heaven by and by
Where no one will be sick or die.

Jesus came down God's love to
  show
To all the people here below;
Then He went back to Heaven, but
  He
Will come again for you and me.

Full of Life

Nell Ford Hann

Everything is full of life
At Easter,
From the robin on the wing,
To the newborn baby lamb.

Everything is full of life
At Easter,
Especially Jesus Christ, my Lord,
Son of the Great I Am!

Easter Smiling Faces

Nell Ford Hann

When we'd make a face,
  Our mother would say,
"Be careful it might
  Freeze that way!"
Wouldn't it be wonderful
  If that was so,
'Cause Easter morning
  Everyone's face is aglow.
Easter Sunday congregation,
  Smiling faces all around;
Greeting old friends and strangers,
  Love and fellowship abound.

Oh, Risen Savior

Saundra Birmingham

Oh, risen Savior
From Easter long ago;
We thank You this day
For Your blessings here below.

We thank You for the cross
You bore to set us free;
We thank You for the blood
You shed out on Calvary.

Lord Jesus, grant us Your Spirit
Again this Easter time;
Please mold each of our lives
In peace and love divine.

Difficult

Good Morning, Easter Day

Helen Kitchell Evans

Good morning, happy Easter Day,
  We're here to welcome you;
  Your message is quite old
  But forever it is new.

Good morning, joyous Easter Day,
  It's resurrection time!
Hear the church bells,
  Oh, hear their lovely chime.

Good morning, blessed Easter Day,
  Christ has risen from the tomb;
He is risen! He is risen!
  Scattered now is all gloom.

It's Because

Helen Kitchell Evans

It's because God sent His son
  To live upon the earth,
It's because of this dear child
  And the miracle of His birth;
It's because He grew to manhood
  Teaching others how to live;
It's because of how He thought
  How He always would forgive.
Yes, it's all because of Jesus
  That every one in every nation
Love and praise the Lord
  And are given the promise of
    salvation.

Crucify Christ

Saundra Birmingham

"Crucify Him! Crucify Him!"
That's what the people said;
"Crucify Him! Crucify Him!
We want Him dead!"

Why crucify Christ?
What on earth had He done?
Who would think of killing
God's only begotten Son?

It seems so hard to believe
Those people were so very mean;
Yet, it is far more amazing
That we today do the same thing.

Oh yes, we crucify Christ
By the things we say and do;
We deny His very existence
When we live anyway we choose
  to.

It seems to be such a shame
When Christ is so rudely
  disdained;
That's why we must seize each
  opportunity
To ensure His glory is reclaimed.

Let us not be guilty
Of crucifying Christ anymore;
Let us keep Him alive
This Easter and forevermore.
    God is so good!

The Most Glorious Time

Lillian Robbins

At sunrise we gather at the church each year
And talk about the empty tomb.
The women were afraid, but the angel said,
"Don't fear, you'll see Him soon."

That must have been the most glorious time
A person could wish to see.
His enemies had thought they defeated Him
When they nailed Him on that tree.

But they were wrong; they could never win
Over God and His magnificent power.
When the Christ had arisen from that earthly grave,
It was surely His finest hour.

Now we sing praises and honor His name,
And pray for our foes and friends.
What a wonderful feeling for us to know
Jesus came to save all men.

If

Saundra Birmingham

Jesus could have come down from that cross
If He had wanted to;
He decided to die of His own will
Just to save me and you.

Jesus could have summoned a band of angels
If He had altogether wanted them;
They would have surely swooped down
To immediately release and rescue Him.

If Jesus had come down from the cross
What would our circumstances now be?
If Jesus had not sacrificed His life for us
What in the world would happen to you and me?

If Jesus had not been buried in that grave
The stone would not have been rolled away;
If Jesus had not proved His resurrection
We would not be celebrating this Easter Day.

Easter Joy

Alta McLain

May the tender joys of Easter
Fill our hearts with praise.
Yes, Jesus died upon the cross,
But arose within three days.
For sinners Jesus bled and died.
For us, our Lord was crucified.

The grave could never hold Him,
The Son of God, at all.
They soon would see and hear
  Him,
And many heard His call
And followed Him just where He
  led.
He had arisen as He said.

Early that first Easter morning
Three who loved Him came
And found the Lord's grave empty,
And gladly praised His name.
Those who seek Jesus on their way
Find and follow Him today.

My Friend

Kimberly Hopkins

I have a friend I hope you know
You've heard about from long ago;
You can see Him in the trees
Over oceans and calming seas.

This is a special time you see
He arose from the dead for you
  and for me;
Caring about us, great and small
He paid the price in full for all.

On a cross on Calvary
He set our sins and burdens free;
Washed in the blood of the lamb
God doesn't see our sins, but sees
  Him.

Thank You Lord we all have a
  friend
That's with us thru the very end;
Rising from death for you and me
We all can have the victory!

An Easter Prayer

Wanda E. Brunstetter

Dear God in Heaven, we bow in
  humble prayer,
Knowing that in everything You
  always care.
We give You our thanks and our
  praise,
For Your kindness shown in so
  many ways.

Dear God in Heaven, we give
  thanks for Your Son,
Through His death on Calvary,
  the victory was won,
He rose again on the first day of
  the week,
He saves the lost and those who
  seek.

He Lives and Gives

Carolyn R. Scheidies

He lives! He lives!
I cry as I bow my head,
Christ Jesus who died,
Upon the cross was crucified,
Rose in victory from the dead.

He cares! He cares!
In gratitude I see,
The baby born in a Bethlehem
  stable,
Is more than a man and able,
To forgive and set me free.

He gives! He gives!
My hands I raise in worship to
  Him,
Who loved me enough
To give release,
Give me life and hope and peace,
As I humbly let Him in.

It's Beginning To Look Like Easter

Nell Ford Hann

It's beginning to look like Easter,
  The lilies are in full bloom;
The robins . . . in their treetops,
  Are chirping their merry tune.

The green has touched the apple
  tree,
  They soon will be in blossom;
Easter's filling every heart,
  From a tadpole to a 'possum.

It's time for bunny rabbits,
  Hopping down their trails;
And little yellow biddies,
  Bursting from their shells.

It's beginning to look like Easter,
  Hear the church bells ring?
It's Resurrection Sunday
  And the pleasing rebirth of spring.

I Will Walk

Carolyn R. Scheidies

I will walk the walk with Jesus,
At work, at school, at play,
For the baby born in Bethlehem
Walks beside me through each
  day.

I will talk each day with Jesus,
Let His Word so live in me,
That the story old is always new,
Christ died for all at Calvary.

I will live each day for Jesus,
I'll be His candle in the night,
Telling one and all about God's
  Son,
Who rose to bring us life.

Yes, I will always live for Jesus,
In all I do and say,
Leading others to my Savior,
To accept His saving grace.

Creation and Me

Carolyn R. Scheidies

How majestic are the Rockies,
Yet Christ is greater far,
And nature but a pale imitation
Of the one who made the stars.

There is nothing wrong with
  enjoying,
The rivers and mountains and
  streams,
As long as they draw us to the
  Creator,
Who died at Calvary.

For Jesus created beauty,
But more He came to die,
And rose in victory from death
  and hell,
Did it all for you and I.

For the God who made the
  universe,
Wants to create in you and me,
Forgiveness, hope and peace and
  love,
And life abundantly.

So at this Easter time,
I worship at His feet,
Thankful that He came in love
And that He came for me.

These Who Loved Him . . .

Kay Hoffman

Their hearts were filled with
  sorrow
As they laid Him in the tomb.
For these who loved the Master
There was hopelessness and
  gloom.

They thought He'd be their earthly
  king.
They could not understand.
He was the Lamb of Sacrifice
In God's redemptive plan.

Peter! John! Come quick and see
  The stone is pushed aside;
Mary's story seemed to them
  As one she had contrived.

But lo, the tomb is open
  The great stone was rolled away,
"Why seekest the living among the
  dead?"
They heard the angel say.

Such news! Was theirs to give that
  day
  To those who thought Him dead;
He lives! He lives! O, wondrous
  joy
He has risen as He said.

Mary, at the Tomb

Kay Hoffman

She came with burial spices
  While the skies yet were gray.
Heart filled with sorrow she
  pondered
  Who would roll the stone away.

But lo, the tomb was open
  The great stone was set aside;
With fearful heart Mary stooped
  And tried to peer inside.

"Why seekest thou the living
  Here among the dead?"
She heard the angel say,
  "He has risen as He said."

When Mary saw her blessed Lord
  Within the garden fair
Her heart was filled with rapture
  As she knelt and worshiped
  there.

The words He spoke to Mary
  He speaks to us today;
"Go tell the others that 'I live'."
  The stone is rolled away.

The Flower's Beauty

Cheryl A. Mariano

Flowers have a beauty, this I don't deny
But they only live a short time, then they fade and quickly die.
God helped me see the flower in a new and different way.
The message is in their color, I pass it on to you today.
The blue ones are the angels, as they watched from Heaven on high
As I left my throne in glory, to go to planet earth to die.
The red ones say I love you, I shed my blood at Calvary.
The green ones simply mean, you'll spend eternity with me.
The yellow says I've risen, I am the Morning Son
I lay no longer in the tomb, my work on earth is done.
The white is for deliverance, I have set the captive free
I have released you from the enemy, you now belong to me.
All the colors in between, the purple, orange, pink
Means I can do way above, all you'll ask or think.
So remember my beloved, when you see a grand bouquet
There is beauty in the flower, and what the flower has to say.

Easter Sunrise Services

Nell Ford Hann

Easter brings out our Sunday best,
Mother makes sure all our clothes
   are pressed,
Sometimes I get a brand new dress,
For Easter sunrise services.

Dad's clean-shaven, hair's freshly
   trimmed,
His dark suit accents how tall and
   slim.
We even waxed the car for him,
For Easter sunrise services.

No teasing from brother, he's on
   his best behavior,
These moments I'm sure my
   mother does savor
As we celebrate the resurrection of
   our Lord and Savior,
At Easter sunrise services.

Guess

Margaret Primrose

I cupped my hands and closed
   them.
"Guess what's inside," I said,
And heard a lot of guesses.
A stone? A spool of thread?

Some sand? A piece of paper?
Is it a stick of gum?
Could it be chocolate candy?
Or maybe it's a crumb.

"It's none of those," said I.
"My hands are Jesus' tomb.
It couldn't hold a risen Lord,
So it's just an empty room."

How wonderful it is
That Jesus lives again!
It makes me want to say,
"I thank You, Lord. Amen."

Our Good Friend

Lillian Robbins

The women were sad
   When they walked down the road
Carrying spices for Jesus;
   Was not a big load.

They had watched Him die,
   Felt pain in their heart,
And because they loved Him
   Wanted to do their part.

Early they arrived
   At the place where He lay,
But His body was gone.
   The angel did say,

"The Lord is alive!
   And before you, He goes.
Just spread the good news
   So everyone knows."

Death could not hold Him.
   God revived Him again.
Now He is our Savior
   And dearest, good friend.

God's Amazing Plan

Lillian Robbins

As the sun rises yonder,
   And a new day begins to dawn,
We remember the glorious Savior
   On that resurrection morn.

It was just the love of Jesus
   That drew Him to that cross.
He willingly suffered misery
   That we would not be lost.

The pain of death He carried
   And called to God above.
In agony of the moment,
   He still revealed His love.

"Forgive them, Father," He pleaded.
   His enemies felt relieved.
They thought they had the victory,
   And they watched His loved ones grieve.

But it wasn't the end for Jesus
   Tho He died with thieves that day.
"Truly this was the Son of God,"
   The guards were heard to say.

As the darkness fell around them,
   And the earth did broadly quake,
The people must have trembled
   Without a sound to make.

Was it all really over,
   The life of this great man,
Or was there something greater
   In God's amazing plan?

The removal of the body
   Of Jesus Christ that day,
By Joseph and Nicodemus
   Who laid the corpse away.

The tomb was sealed and guarded,
   The Sabbath drawing near,
No further preparations,
   For one they held so dear.

But the women's plans were ready.
   At the end of Holy day,
They would return to see their Jesus
   In the tomb where He was laid.

In the dawning of the morning
   When they quietly made their way,
They knew not what had happened
   On that resurrection day.

They were frightened by the angel,
   What astounding news they heard!
From the grave He had risen!
   It was the angel's revealing word.

Death had not been victorious.
   Jesus' enemies could not win.
The power of God was greater.
   His Son had conquered sin!

And now this day of memory
   When we see again that time,
We can claim His saving power.
   Thank God, the Savior's mine.

Easter Prayer

Lillian Robbins

As we gather to celebrate Easter,
Dear Father and God above,
We are bathed in your holy
    presence
And your Son's amazing love.

Help us, Lord, to remember
That lonely day He spent
As the sentence to Him was given
And up Calvary's hill He went.

Show us again the nail prints
In His hands and feet that day.
The thorns upon His brow,
Like a criminal He went His way.

Permit us to feel His anguish,
The sorrow of all those sins
He took upon His shoulders
That man with Christ might win.

Give us grateful measure
To reflect the life He lived
As a perfect and Godly example,
And in death His all did give.

Teach us now His manner
Of compassion and faith and love
That we might grow in spirit,
In likeness of the Son above.

Supply us with such motives,
  A spirit of forgiveness to gain
That hate and prejudice be con-
    quered
With peace for man to man.

Direct us, Lord, in righteousness
To seek and live Your way,
To renew our vows this morning
On this great Easter day.

Accept our praise and worship,
With You we, too, proclaim
Resurrection and salvation
By the Son who bears Your
    name.

We thank You, Father and Jesus,
And humbly bow to pray.
Lead us in all our trials,
And forgive our sinful ways.

Hallelujah! He is risen!
And the earth He now has left
Cleansing every spot and blemish
In His glorious triumphant death.

We praise His name forever,
Our lives to Him we give
That we, too, might be risen
In eternity with You to live.

Now *help us, show us, permit us,
give us, teach us, supply us,
direct us, accept us* and finally
bring us into Your heavenly
    home
That we might celebrate eternally
the loving power of the resur-
    rection morn.
In the name of the risen Savior, we
pray. Amen.

Exercises

We Are Here

Helen Kitchell Evans

Girl: I'm a little girl,
Boy: I'm a little boy;
Both: We are here
   To bring you Easter joy.

(They hold up a sign that says "Happy Easter.")

Springtime In the Air

Helen Kitchell Evans

Child 1
Small flowers popping up,
It's such a lovely day!

Child 2
Each little flower looks at me,
Each one seems to say,

Child 3
"Hello, there, I'm here to tell you
That springtime's in the air.

Child 4
That the love of Easter
Can be seen everywhere."

All
Be glad! Be glad! It's Easter!
Christ lives! He lives! He lives!
Christ, our Lord, our Savior,
With love each sin forgives.

"Easter Is . . ."

Saundra Birmingham

Speaker #1
Easter is joy
Easter is cheer;
Easter Sunday
Is oh, so dear.

Speaker #2
Easter is love
Easter is life;
Easter is Jesus
Making a sacrifice.

Speaker #3
Easter is completely His
Because He lives!

"He is not here: for he is risen as he said. Come, see the place where the Lord lay.
-- Matthew 28:6

His Touch

Carolyn R. Scheidies

For 4 individuals or groups

Lord, touch my eyes *(Indicate eyes.)*
And help me see
All the blessings
That you have for me.

Touch my mouth *(Touch mouth.)*
And make it so
Not complaints, but
Only praise and worship flows.

Touch my body *(Put hand on head.)*
That I might know
The love of He who died
To make me whole.

Lord Jesus, touch my trembling heart, *(Cover heart.)*
With courage to share what you've done for me,
The message of forgiveness,
That others too may be set free.

Song: "Take My Life and Let It Be"

Our God Is

Carolyn R. Scheidies

Our God is good. He does not change,
Through time and space, remains the same. Hebrews 13:8

Our God is true,
He's always there for me and you. John 14:6

Our God is just and right.
Though He must punish evil and wrong, He offers us His light. Romans 6:23

Our God is love. His only son He gave,
To die upon the cross, you and I to save. John 3:16-17

Our God is strong. He conquered sin,
Left death behind that you and I, might freely come to Him. John 5:24

All: Psalm 145:3
Song: "Great Is the Lord" *(optional)*

He is Risen

His Love

Lillian Robbins

First Child
April showers bring May flowers,
But God brings the greatest joy.

Second Child
Not just in spring when birds all sing;
Jesus loves every girl and boy.

Third Child
As with the dawn of that early morn,
His love is here in my heart.
(Hand over heart.)

Fourth Child
He arose from the grave so I can be saved,
And never from Him depart.

Drawn to the Cross

Helen Kitchell Evans

Child 1
We are drawn to the cross
As we worship this day
For Christians all know
Christ died in this way.

Child 2
He died on the cross
To save you and me;
Because He gave His life then
Salvation is free.

Child 3
He only asks we have faith,
And live right each day
That we think of others
And that daily we pray.

All
He died on a day
Filled with great sadness;
From the tomb He arose
To a day filled with gladness.

E-A-S-T-E-R Message

Carolyn R. Scheidies

For six, each holds up a letter.

E is for **each** wrong we do,
  Each pain, each hurt, each lie.
A is for God's **answer**
  In sending Jesus Christ.
S is for God's **Son**
  Who died at Calvary.
T is for the **tree**
  On which He died for you and me.
E is for **each** and **every one** of us
  For whom Jesus came,
R is for His **resurrection**
  Rising again from death and the grave.

All: This then the message of Easter,
  Jesus died and rose for you and me.
  Offering forgiveness to each heart,
  And with His love, His peace.

W-E-L-C-O-M-E

Dixie Phillips

Children enter and stand in a straight line across the stage. Their cards are turned so the congregation doesn't see the letters. This could be used for any special holiday play. Just fill in the blank.

Child 1: *(turns W card)* **W** means welcome. We are so glad you came.
Child 2: *(turns E card)* **E** means everyone. Jesus loves us all the same.
Child 3: *(turns L card)* **L** means love, the kind that Jesus gives.
Child 4: *(turns C card)* **C** means cross, Jesus died but now He lives!
Child 5: *(turns O card)* **O** means "OH!" We're up in front of you!
Child 6: *(turns M card)* **M** means Mommy, she's proud of what I do.
Child 7: *(turns E card)* **E** means end, that's all we have to say.
Unison: Welcome everyone to our _____ play!

What Did I See?

Margaret Primrose

First Child
What did I see in the mall today?
A hat that was wearing a big
    bouquet;
Easter dresses, flowered and frilly;
A make-believe rabbit acting silly;

Jelly bean eggs, and a chocolate,
    too,
That mashed in my hand and
    turned to goo;
Babies crying; children pouting;
Moms who wanted to end the
    outing.

My feet began to feel like lead.
I'm glad I'm not a quadruped.
If Easter is only a trip to the mall,
I'd rather just forget it all.

Second Child
What did I see in my church today?
Parents and children coming to pray;
Sunbeams warming an Easter lily,
Though the weather outside was
    windy and chilly;

Teachers who love to make learning
    a game
And lead in praising God's
    wonderful name;
The choir that marches down the
    aisle;
A pastor who tells us with a smile

That Jesus died and rose again
To bring us His peace and save us
    from sin.
Today I learned that He did it for me,
So Easter's as special as it can be.

I Can Praise

Dixie Phillips

(Three children enter carrying palm branches.)
Child 1: Hosannas filled the village square,
As Jesus entered there.
Child 2: The little children's voices did ring,
As His praises they did sing!
Child 3: I can still praise Him today,
In my own special way.
Unison: Hosanna! *(Wave palms.)* We love You Jesus!

We All Saw It

Dolores Steger

A choral reading, children may wear costumes.

All: Yes! We all saw it! We know that it's true!
Just hear now our story; we'll tell it to you!
Child 1: Joseph of Arimathea is my name;
To the foot of the cross so sadly I came;
I watched the Lord die and, humbly, I gave
A place for His body to rest, in a cave.
Child 2: Mighty centurion, that's who am I;
I guarded the tomb under dark, clouded sky;
Suddenly, oh, the whole world seemed to shake;
I fell to my knees; I could not keep awake.
Child 3: Mary I am and I went Sunday morn
To care for the Master whose body was torn;
The boulder that sealed the tomb where He laid
Had been moved; He was missing; I ran, so afraid.
Child 4: Mary of Magdalene, I went there, too;
The tomb, it was empty! What was I to do?
Then, in the garden, a soft voice I heard,
The Lord's saying, "Mary, I live! Spread the word!"
Child 5: Thomas they call me; I couldn't suppose
That Jesus, the Savior who died, had arose;
But I felt His wounds and knew it was so;
Now, to the whole world I must tell what I know.
All: Christ lives and He's with you, if you so choose;
The truth we have told you, now go! Spread the news!

The Living Christ

Iris Gray Dowling

(Each child holds a letter spelling the word "CHRIST".)

C hrist was born in Bethlehem—
His life to give for sinful men.
H is own sacrifice on Calv'ry
Was planned by God to make us free.
R isen early Easter Day
He met disciples on His way.
I n Heaven Jesus went to stay,
But He'll return to earth some day.
S aved ones watch in fervent prayer,
Wait to join their Lord in the air.
T ogether we shall rise
To that meeting in the skies.

Easter Again

Helen Kitchell Evans

Choir I:	Happy Easter!
Choir II:	Joyful day!
Chorus:	Again, again it's Easter.
Choir I:	People gather everywhere
Choir II:	Offering up an Easter prayer.
Chorus:	Again, again it's Easter.
Choir I:	Christ arose on this day,
Choir II:	In the tomb He did not stay,
Chorus:	Again, again it's Easter.
Choir I:	The earth relives this wondrous story
Choir II:	Of Christ who died and arose to glory,
Chorus:	Again, again, it's Easter!

If I Had Lived When Jesus Lived

Amy Houts

This drama is designed for easy production. Spotlights focus on the message of each part. A few props are needed, as are some period costumes. Children should be set up on stage and ready for action when it is time. The spotlight will be the cue for their part to start. Jesus and the narrator are present in more than one part.

Characters
Narrator
Fisherman #1
Fisherman #2
Fisherman #3
Woman
Jesus
Child #1
Child #2
Mary—mother of Jesus
Mary Magdalene

Props: fishing net, boat and seas made from cardboard, treats for crowd, tables with coins, a door that can slam, bread, goblet, cross.

Time: When Jesus lived and present day

Costumes: All should be robes, tunics, and sandals such as were worn in ancient Rome. Women should have their heads covered.

Narrator: If I had lived when Jesus lived
I know I would have followed Him
And listened to His every word,
Called Him friend,
Called Him Lord,
If I had lived when Jesus lived.
Fisherman #1: When He calmed the stormy seas
(Kneels.) I would have been down on my knees.
Fisherman #2: Then I would leave my fishing nets *(Throws nets down.)*
And would have helped Him feed the crowd.
(Goes down to audience and hands out treats.)
Fisherman #3: I'd smile and sing His name aloud!
If I had lived when Jesus lived.
Woman: I would have watched Him heal a man
I would have heard Him say "I AM."

Narrator:	And when the money changers roared
	(Jesus turns over tables.)
	The tables toppled to the floor.
	I'd follow Him and slam the door *(Slams door.)*
	If I had lived when Jesus lived.
Child #1:	I would have broken bread with Him
	(Tear bread and share drink with Jesus.)
	Passed the cup, lived the grace
	Of being in that holy place.
Child #2:	Best of all the stories told
	I could have listened 'til I was old
	(Child looks up at Jesus.)
	If I had lived when Jesus lived.
Mary:	I'd cry to see Him bear His cross. *(Jesus carries cross.)*
	Thinking then that all is lost.
	Watching, waiting the third day
	As He arose and went His way. *(Jesus rises and walks.)*
Mary Magdalene:	I would have witnessed to the crowd.
	"I've seen Him!" I would shout out loud.
	If I had lived when Jesus lived.
Narrator:	Jesus is alive today
	In the same yet different way.
	So you could say my story's true
	We all live when Jesus lived.

The Cross

Dolores Steger

All:	Look at the cross! Tell me, what do you see?
Child 1:	I see a Savior who died just for me;
Child 2:	I see friend Jesus who loves and who cares;
Child 3:	I see a crown that, in Heaven, He wears;
Child 4:	I see our Lord; from a cave He arose;
Child 5:	I see His face and the care that it shows;
Child 6:	I see love's symbol; before it I bow;
Child 7:	I see the One who is God with us now;
All:	Look at the cross! Praise the Lord! Hear us say,
	God's blessing came to us on that Easter Day!

Symbols for Jesus' Life

Dolores Steger

An Easter play in one act for children of all ages.

Characters
Six youths *(speaking parts)* dressed in casual clothes
Six to twelve younger children *(nonspeaking parts)* dressed in casual clothes. Each younger child to carry 1 "egg" sign, if working with 12 children; 2 signs per child, if less than 12
Jesus, dressed in robe

Props and set requirements: Minimal; kitchen of a house, enhance as desired
Required: table for coloring Easter eggs, 12 plastic eggs, materials for simulated egg dyeing (cups, paints, crayons, etc.), 12 large Easter eggs cut from poster board on which have been drawn the 12 symbols mentioned in the play (one symbol per board: star, lighted candle, fish, shell, wheat, grapes, crown of thorns, cross, dove, rock, butterfly, lily)

Music: Choir or tape

Time: The present

Scriptures taken from the New International Version.

Kitchen of a house; six youths are working at a table coloring Easter eggs. Jesus is standing off to one side, looking on. Music plays "O How I Love Jesus"; music stops as Youth 1 speaks.

Youth 1: I'm really glad we decided to start coloring our Easter eggs early this year. When we're rushed, the eggs just don't turn out as pretty.
Youth 2: You're so right! I only wish we could think of something different to put on the eggs this time. Chicks and bunnies and ducks are fine, but you get tired of them after a while.
Youth 3: I know what you mean. Let's try to think of something original.
Youth 4: How about glitter? The eggs would really sparkle and shine then.

Youth 5: Or we could use some neon paint. Then the eggs would glow in the dark.
Youth 6: Not bad! We could also use colored glue and stick on bits of cloth and paper to give the eggs a three-dimensional look.
Youth 2: Or we could—
Youth 1 *(interrupting):* Wait! Wait! I've got it! I know something we could put on them that we'd never get tired of! We could put symbols for Jesus on our eggs! After all, He's like a friend who's with us all the time and His resurrection is the reason we celebrate Easter!
All: Symbols?
Youth 1: Sure! Sure! You know! Emblems! Signs! Things you see every day that remind you of Jesus!
All: Terrific idea!
Youth 3: Yes! Yes! And you know what! We could start out with symbols that remind us of His birth and work all the way through His life on earth to the resurrection!
All: Now that's thinking!
Youth 4: All right! All right! Pass out the eggs! Let's decide what symbols we're going to use and get started!
(Music plays "I Love to Tell the Story" as they pass out eggs and begin working on them. Music subsides as Youth 6 speaks.)
Youth 6: I think I'll start out with a star on one egg and a candle on the other. They're both reminders of Jesus and they're both reminders of His birth.
(Jesus moves forward, speaks to the audience and to the Youths, then returns to his previous position on stage.)
Jesus: I am the light of the world. Whoever follows me will never walk in darkness, but will have the light of life. (John 8:12)
(Two children enter carrying poster board eggs, one with candle, one with star; they walk in front of the table where Youths are working, circle around it, showing eggs to audience, and stand behind the table.)
Youth 5: I'm going to use a fish and a shell on my eggs. When we see them, we think of Jesus walking along the shore of Galilee. They remind us of His ministry and how He brought disciples to God and preached along the way.
(Jesus comes forward as before and speaks.)
Jesus: Come, follow me . . . and I will make you fishers of men. (Matthew 4:19)
(Music plays "I Will Make You Fishers of Men". Jesus returns to previous position. Two children with poster eggs, one shell, one fish, enter, pass in front of table, circle it showing eggs to audience, and stand next to the first two children. Music diminishes as Youth 1 speaks.)
Youth 1: I'm so happy! This project is really going great!

All: Sure is!
Youth 3: I'm glad we thought of this idea.
Youth 4: Well, I've decided what I'm going to do. I'm going to put wheat on one of my eggs and grapes on the other—you know—to stand for Jesus and for the last days He spent with His disciples on earth. Like in the upper room when they shared bread and wine together.
(Jesus comes forward and speaks.)
Jesus: Take and eat; this is my body. . . . Drink from it, all of you. This is my blood of the covenant, which is poured out for many for the forgiveness of sins. (Matthew 26:26-28)
(Jesus returns to previous position; two more children enter with poster board eggs, one with wheat, one with grapes, walk around table as before and stand next to the children already there.)
Youth 5: There sure are a lot of symbols of Christ in this world and you never seem to get tired of looking at them. They just keep on reminding you that Jesus is everywhere.
All: You said it.
Youth 3: Now, let's see. We've done His birth and His ministry and His last days with the disciples. I know. I'll do two symbols that always remind people of Jesus—and also of the crucifixion. I'll do a cross on one of my eggs and a crown of thorns on the other.
All: Great! Super!
(Jesus moves forward and speaks.)
Jesus: Be faithful . . . and I will give you the crown of life. . . . And anyone who does not take his cross and follow me is not worthy of me. (Revelation 2:10; Matthew 10:38)
(Music plays "Standing on the Promises." Jesus returns to his place on stage. Two children enter with appropriate poster eggs and stand next to other children with posters. Music diminishes as Youth 1 speaks.)
Youth 1 *(to Youth 2)*: What are you going to do?
Youth 2: I was thinking about it. You know, they call Jesus "The Rock" sometimes and, when they buried Him, they sealed His tomb with a big rock. So, I think I'll put a rock on one of my eggs. On the other, I'm going to put a dove. That's a symbol of Jesus and it also stands for the peace that surrounded Him in the tomb and for His spirit waiting to rise.
Youth 1: A rock! A dove! Good idea, but they're hard to draw.
Youth 2: I know, but I'll just do my best.
(Jesus steps forward and speaks.)
Jesus: The Lord is my rock, my fortress and my deliverer; my God is my rock, in whom I take refuge. . . . Oh, that I had the wings of a dove! I would fly away and be at rest. (2 Samuel 22:2; Psalm 55:6)

(Jesus returns to previous stage position. Two children enter with egg symbols and proceed as previous children did.)
Youth 2 *(to Youth 1)*: And what are you going to do?
Youth 1: I've been thinking about this for some time now. I think I'll do a lily and a butterfly. They're both symbols of Christ and they also stand for the resurrection and for the promise of birth and rebirth and that's what Easter should mean to all of us!
(Jesus moves forward and speaks.)
Jesus: I am the resurrection and the life. He who believes in me will live, even though he dies; and whoever lives and believes in me will never die. (John 11:25, 26)
(Music plays "He Keeps Me Singing". Jesus returns to previous position on stage. Last two children enter with poster eggs and join other children on stage. When children are in position, Youth move away from table to front of stage; children with posters move to each side of Youth. Music stops as Youth 6 speaks.)
Youth 6: Let's look at our symbols!
All Youths: Wheat, grapes, the lily and the fish,
　　　　　　　　The dove, the butterfly,
　　　　　　　　Are living symbols of the Lord,
　　　　　　　　The Christ we deify.

　　　　　　　　We celebrate His presence with
　　　　　　　　A shell, a star, a light;
　　　　　　　　A cross, a crown, a rock
　　　　　　　　Remind us of His might.

　　　　　　　　Reflect on them this Easter time,
　　　　　　　　And all the joy they bring,
　　　　　　　　These symbols of Christ, the Lord,
　　　　　　　　Our risen Savior, King!

All Youths and Children: Easter Blessings!

(Music plays "Christ the Lord Is Risen Today." Youths and children take curtain call, bow, exit.)

Mother's Day

Wishes to My Mother

Iris Gray Dowling

Mother, my thoughts are of you
On this very special day;
You deserve much happiness
As you walk along life's way.

I Can

Dixie Phillips

I can say my A B C's!
I can say, "My mommy sure loves
 me!"

A Special Blessing

Dolores Steger

Mommy, Mama, Mother, Ma,
By any name, know what you are?
A special blessing, yes, it's true,
I feel God's love when I'm near
 you.

Sweet Smelling Mom

Iris Gray Dowling

No coin could ever buy
 The joy that I have known.
There's no mother like mine
 Who smells like fresh cologne.

I Can Help

Helen Kitchell Evans

My mother does so much for me
I am small as you can see.
But I can help in my own way
By minding mother both night and
 day.

Must Be

Helen Kitchell Evans

How can mothers always be
Forever right? They are you see.
At least it seems so to me.
Must be that God just speaks to
 mothers
More special than He does to
 others.

In All I Do

Helen Kitchell Evans

I help my dear Mother,
I *work* and *work* and *work*!
I dust the chairs and tables,
No duty do I shirk.

I help all that I can,
I wash the dishes, too;
I tell you I am *mighty good*
 (Teasing, looks at
 congregation and smiles.)
In everything I do.

34

A Better Place

Helen Kitchell Evans

If every home could have
A mother full of grace
The world would surely be
A much, much better place.

There's the mother that I have
   (Points to mother.)
She fills our home with love
Because she prays to God
For His blessings from above.

Great Mother's Day

Helen Kitchell Evans

I want to be like mother
I know she was quite good
Because my grandmother told me
She always did the things she
   should.

I try to please my mother
In every single way
So she will really have
One great Mother's Day.

For Mother With Love

Three Little Words

Lillian Robbins

Three little words,
   "I love you,"
   Have been said many times.

I want to say them
   To my mother dear
   Now in this little rhyme.

You're the greatest!
   No doubt about it,
   I know it is the truth.

Now it's my turn
   Just to say, Mom,
   I certainly, surely, truly, really,
   absolutely, do love you!
   (Throws a kiss to Mom.)

When Push Comes to Shove

Donna Colwell Rosser

Everyday should be Mother's Day,
   But it seems it seldom comes.
Everyday, we're thankful,
   But infrequent are the drums
Pounding out the message
   That mothers should get thanks.
Unusual is the fanfare
   Celebrating the ranks
Of dedicated mothers—
   Of which you are the elite.
As a mom, you are a magician,
   For raising children is a feat;
Requiring push, some pull,
   Some holding back, some shove.
So our thanks are more than
   politeness,
   They are visceral feelings of love.

The Gift of Love

Dolores Steger

Mothers are like packages,
I do believe it's so,
Each is a different size and shape,
Each has a different glow.
In one way, though, they are alike;
Give thanks to God above,
In each one of these packages,
He's placed the gift of love.

Thank You, Father, On Mother's Day

Nell Ford Hann

I thank You, Father,
  On Mother's Day,
    Because there is no other;
    For . . . Lord . . . I am so
grateful,
  You created
    My dear Mother!

Mother's Day Card

Nell Ford Hann

I went to the store
  To buy a Mother's Day card;
For a special mom
  That works very hard.
They had mushy-gushy
  And gooey ones, too;
But none, thought I,
  As sweet as you.
So I came back home,
  And decided right then,
I'd make Mom a card,
  But where do I begin?
If I decorated with red hearts,
  I know Valentine,
Would be the thing,
  That would come to your mind.
You'd think it was Christmas,
  If I drew a green tree,
So I just wrote, "Hi, Mom,
  I love you . . . from me!"

Mother's Day

Kay Hoffman

One of the warmest pleasures
  In the month of May each year
Is when the children gather round
  To honor mother dear.

In all the hurried pace
  Of our living day by day
We oft neglect warm, loving words
  Our hearts would have us say.

A flower or a special card
  Will add to mother's bliss,
But sweeter still, "I love you,
  Mom,"
Delivered with a kiss.

God bless all mothers on this day
  And fill each heart with cheer,
But let's remember mother
  Each day throughout the year.

Mom Brings Joy

Lillian Robbins

My brother likes trucks and great
    big balls,
And puzzles and games are fun.
But what do I love most of all?
    You know it must be Mom.

She makes delicious lunches
    And cakes with chocolate tops.
And I know just what she means
    When she yells at me, "Now
    stop!"

I see tears in her eyes and wonder,
    Have I been all that bad?
That her happy face has faded
    And I see a face so sad.

Most of the time she smiles and
    sings,
    Brings joy in all our house.
I cuddle up in her loving arms,
    For a minute, still as a mouse.

When school is over, and I've
    finished with play,
    In my "jammies" I'm ready for
    bed,
Mom reads and prays and gives
    me hugs,
    "I love you, Dear," she says.

Thanks for Mom

Margaret Primrose

My mother likes to cook
    And helps me feed the cat.
She doesn't care for T-ball
    But cheers for me when I bat.

And just because she loves me,
    Sometimes we take a walk
To see the neighbor's flowers.
    At night we often talk

About how Jesus loves us
    And hears us when we pray.
I thank Him for my mom
    On this happy Mother's Day.

God's Gift

Helen Kitchell Evans

I thank God for my mother
    As I'm sure do each of you;
A wonderful loving mother
    Who loves you your whole life
    through.

When you are a small child
    She watches you with care;
When you are older
    You know she will be there.

A mother is God's gift
    To each of us right here;
Always willing, always ready
    To fill our lives with cheer.

Mama's Bible

Dixie Phillips

I found it in my mama's Bible and I know it's true,
It's that "Old-time religion," nothing else will do!
I found it in my mama's Bible, it's all that I need,
If I read it carefully and it's words I heed!
Whenever I am troubled and don't know what to do,
I go to my mama's Bible, 'cause it's my Bible too!

My Mom Is Not

Dixie Phillips

Child #1: My mom is not as rich as a royal queen,
She is very sweet and never ever mean!
Child #2: My mom is not as famous as a movie star,
But to me *(point to self)* she's the most famous person by far!
Child #3: My mom is not president, I'm thankful for that, *(wipe brow, whew!)*
Everyone would have to know the name of our cat!
Child #4: These are just a few things our moms are not,
But there is one thing she has that no one else has got—
Unison: ME! *(point to self)*

My Mother

Iris Gray Dowling

(Exercise for a class; four single parts and class group.)

Child #1: Nothing on earth can compare
Group: With my mother.
Child #2: No one has devoted love
Group: Like my mother.
Child #3: Many blessings God gave me
Group: Came from my mother.
Child #4: I've tried to find the words to say—
Group: Thank You, God, for my mother.

M - O - T - H - E - R

Iris Gray Dowling

(Six children each hold a letter to spell "MOTHER".)

M   is for Mother,
        Who gives so much for those God puts in her care.
O   is for Others—
        For whom she spends much time in prayer.
T   is for Tell,
        She tells the Gospel story of God above.
H   is for Heart,
        Where mother hides the verses of love.
E   is for Eager,
        That's the way she works for every one.
R   is for Righteous—
        How God sees mother when she receives His Son.

Happy Mother's Day

Kimberly J. Hopkins

Happy Mother's Day all year through.
Celebrating Mother's Day is for mothers like you!
You love everybody and everybody loves you.
You are so thoughtful and so true blue.

You have the art of being able to listen
Not being judgmental and unforgiving,
With a gentle hug and a tender kiss
You make the bad turn into bliss.

It's a comfort knowing we have loved ones like you
Who are praying for us and others too!
Never thinking of only Y-O-U
Or what people should or should not do.

So happy Mother's Day for all you do
Being a loving mother and great friend too!
Some day I hope to be blessed like you
By having people who love you like we all do!

A Wonderful Mother

Lillian Robbins

A Mother's Day reading for youth or young adult.

She is loving enough to shower her children with devotion
  and wise enough to know love demands discipline.
She is patient enough to explain rules more than once
  and firm enough to enforce them.
She is kind enough to speak softly
  and in control enough to prove her authority.
She is defensive enough to protect her offspring
  and fair enough to acknowledge the rights of others.
She is compassionate enough to feel what her children feel
  and strong enough to help them look beyond shadows.
She is protective enough to watch over her children
  and wise enough to know she can't protect them always.
She is unselfish enough to give generously
  and smart enough to teach that giving is a two way street.
She is aggressive enough to give the best to her children
  and realistic enough to know that's more than money.
She is loving enough for each individual child
  and convincing enough to teach them to share.
She is forgiving enough to restore broken spirits
  and constant enough to lead to a better path.
She is confident enough to raise children with moral values
  and trusting enough to permit them to make decisions.
She is mature enough to cut the apron strings
  and supportive enough to enable her child to start a family of her own.
Thank you, Mother, for being all these things wrapped up in one loving
  bundle of feminine charm. Have a Happy Mother's Day!

Supper Invitation

Dixie Phillips

I'm thankful for the sun that shines so bright!
I'm thankful for the moon that glows at night!
I'm thankful for the rain that gives the grass a drink.
I'm thankful for my teacher, she really makes me think!
I have so many things that I am thankful for,
Do you think you can stand to hear just one more?
I'm very thankful for my mother so divine.
I'm sure she would love to feed you supper sometime!
So, happy Mother's Day Mom, *(Wave.)* don't you work too hard!
There's only _____ people coming to picnic in our yard!
(Put number of people from your church.)

Wrinkle

Dixie Phillips

My mother found a wrinkle on her pretty face,
She couldn't believe it and thought it was a disgrace.
I quickly assured her that she looked just fine,
And the reason for the wrinkle might be mine.
I reminded her of the time I cut my own hair,
And I tried to glue it back with super glue, right there. *(Pat head.)*
Then there was the day my report card came,
I never thought my mother would ever be the same. *(Shake head.)*
I certainly have provided free shock therapy,
Yes, the reason for that wrinkle just might be me.
Like the time I tried to flush disposable diapers down the commode,
Or the time I brought home the snake I found on the road!
Then there was the time I kind of punched my brother,
And the time my rabbit, Snuggles became a mother.
She only had twelve bunnies,
My father though it was funny.
Maybe my daddy is part of the reason too.
Maybe he caused wrinkle number two.
Always remember these are the best years of your life.
How about the time I played in my sandbox with your favorite knife.
A wrinkle's not so bad on your skin so fair.
I'm just surprised you don't have premature gray hair!

41

Father's Day

This Is

Dixie Phillips

This is the day that we've set aside,
To thank our fathers for how hard
   they've tried,
To teach us all the way we should
   go,
To live for Jesus, our Savior to
   know.

Luckiest Kid

Dixie Phillips

I'm the luckiest kid in the world
   today,
Cause I get to stand up here and
   say,
My dad is the best, I'm sure you'll
   agree,
The luckiest kid is me...Me...ME!!!

When Father Reads the Bible

Ada E. Tomlinson

When father reads the Bible,
Please listen as he reads;
It's God speaking to His children,
It's a message each little one
   needs.

Happy Father's Day

Ada E. Tomlinson

We wish a happy Father's Day,
To every father here,
We hope you'll come back next
   Sunday
And not wait until next year!

Super Dad

Iris Gray Dowling

God gave to me a super dad—
A cheerful man with lots of love.
He cares about each one of us,
And shows us joy from God
   above.

I Salute You

Margaret Primrose

A soldier in the army
Puts his hand above his eye
To show he has respect
When a colonel passes by.

My daddy's not a colonel—
For that I'm sometimes glad—
But he deserves respect from me,
So I salute you, Dad.

My Best Pal

Phyllis C. Michael

I have a rake and hoe you see,
And so has Daddy, just like me!
He lets me help him every night,
We keep the garden clean all right.

It's fun to play with boys all day
But when Dad's home from work,
    well—say,
I'd rather be with him by far
Than any place the fellas are.

He's My Dad

Nell Ford Hann

Over and over he'll tell us,
    Of days when he was young;
Or what he wants to say is . . .
    On the tip of his tongue,
His song of life and love
    Is still being sung . . .
        He's my Dad!

Though his dark hair has turned,
    As white as the snow,
His determined quick pace,
    Is now turtle slow,
He still has a chuckle,
    That comes up from his toes . . .
        He's my Dad!

His brow is deeply etched
    From trials he has weathered,
His face is all worn,
    Like age-old shoe leather,
But the hours just fly . . . when
    We're out fishing together . . .
        He's my Dad!

Too Little

Helen Kitchell Evans

What do you mean, "Too little"?
Of course I'm little, but see
I can say "Happy Father's Day."
And fill his heart with glee.

My Dad

Lillian Robbins

My dad likes the golf course,
    And that's not nearly all.
We have fun times together.
    He can easily dunk a ball.

And everyone who knows him
    Can very quickly see
He's great with all his children
    And loves his family.

I know my dad's a Christian,
    Not just when the day is Sunday.
He teaches me to live right,
    Even when it's only Monday.

At night when it's time for sleeping,
    I feel safe 'cause Dad is here.
He says he'll always love me.
    It's cool to have him near.

And Dad, you're the greatest!
    (Points to Dad.)

It's Father's Day

Lillian Robbins

It's Father's Day,
   The people say,
   And this you all should know.

My dad's the greatest!
   NUMBER ONE!
   And you can see it's so.

He's a busy man
   At church and work,
   But spends good time with me.

We camp a bit
   And play some ball
   And he reads good books to me.

When things happen
   I don't understand,
   And I'm puzzled at what life means,

My dad knows
   Just what to say
   And calms my fears it seems.

I just wish
   For all the guys
   To have a dad like mine.

The world would be
   A better place
   And the streets be free from crime.

Thank you, Dad,
   For all you do
   To bring us so much joy.

When all is said,
   There's just one thing,
   I'm really a lucky boy.

My Dad's Special

Lillian Robbins

(Use appropriate description.)

My dad is short
   And has red hair,
   And that's just great with me.

You can't judge a man
   By the color of his hair,
   Or if he's six foot three.

My dad's real special
   To all us kids.
   He fills our lives with love.

He teaches us daily
   And shows us how
   To live for God above.

I wouldn't trade him
   For all the world
   'Cause no one can take his
   place.

If a contest begins
   For the greatest dad,
   My dad will win the race.

Happiness and Cheer

Helen Kitchell Evans

Fathers are proud of pretty girls
  I'm pretty as you can see
    (pause, smile)
But that isn't the reason
  My father is proud of me.

He's proud of me because
  I listen and I mind;
Also, because I'm learning
  To be a person who is kind.

I'll just keep right on trying
  As I grow from year to year
So my growing up will bring him
  Happiness and cheer.

My Dad's the Best

Lillian Robbins

In the morning my dad wakes me
  up
  And says it's time for school.
He fixes my breakfast, packs my
  lunch,
  And reminds me of all his rules.

When he has time, he plays with me
  And shows me lots of things.
And when he tucks me in at night,
  Would you believe, he actually
  sings?

We pray to God and he always
  says,
  "Now, son, you have a good
  rest."
Nobody has to tell me the truth,
  I know my dad's the best.

It's Dad

Margaret Primrose

It's Dad who oils the mower
  And helps me fly my kite.
It's Dad who trims the hedge
  To make it look just right.

He taught me how to fish
  And where to dig for worms.
He will share a sticky gumdrop
  And never mention germs.

So now it is time to tell him,
  "I'm glad to be your son.
Of all the dads I've ever met,
  To me you are number one."

Isn't It Great

Helen Kitchell Evans

Child 1:	Isn't it great we have a day
Child 2:	To honor fathers everywhere?
Child 1:	Fathers who love us so much,
Child 2:	Fathers who really, really care.
Child 1:	So here's a happy greeting,
Child 2:	To all the fathers here:
Both:	We hope our little greeting
	Will fill your day with cheer.

My Daddy Has . . .

Dixie Phillips

Child 1: My daddy has big muscles just like Superman.
  (Child dressed like Superman.)
Child 2: My daddy can build anything, he always has a plan.
  (Child carrying a hammer.)
Child 3: My daddy can drive us just about anywhere.
  (Child carrying a map.)
Child 4: He never has to stop and ask how to get there!
  (Child holding poster that says, "Mommy calls him Mr. Know-it-all.")
Child 5: My mommy says my daddy treats her like a queen.
  (Child dressed up like a queen.)
Child 6: If I don't mind the first time, he's just a teeny-tiny mean.
  (Child shows teeny-tiny with fingers.)
Unison: So Daddy here's your reward for being Father of the Year,
  Lots of candy kisses to bring you lots of cheer!
  (Children throw candy kisses.)

A Father's Instruction

John and Audra Parker

Scriptures are from Proverbs 4:1-27, New International Version.

Man 1: Listen, my sons, to a father's instruction; pay attention and gain understanding. I give you sound learning, so do not forsake my teaching. When I was a boy in my father's house, still tender, and an only child of my mother, he taught me and said,

Man 2: "Lay hold of my words with all your heart;
    keep my commands and you will live.
Get wisdom, get understanding;
    do not forget my words or swerve from them.
Do not forsake wisdom, and she will protect you;
    love her, and she will watch over you.
Wisdom is supreme; therefore get wisdom.
    Though it cost all you have, get understanding.
Esteem her, and she will exalt you;
    embrace her, and she will honor you.
She will set a garland of grace on your head
    and present you with a crown of splendor."

Man 1: Listen, my son, accept what I say, and the years of your life will be many. I guide you in the way of wisdom and lead you along straight paths. When you walk, your steps will not be hampered; when you run, you will not stumble.

Man 2: Hold on to instruction, do not let it go;
    guard it well, for it is your life.
Do not set foot on the path of the wicked
    or walk in the way of evil men.
Avoid it, do not travel on it;
    turn from it and go on your way.
For they cannot sleep till they do evil;
    they are robbed of slumber till they make someone fall.
They eat the bread of wickedness
    and drink the wine of violence.
The path of the righteous is like the first gleam of dawn,
    shining ever brighter till the full light of day.

> But the way of the wicked is like deep darkness;
> they do not know what makes them stumble.

Man 1: My son, pay attention to what I say; listen closely to my words. Do not let them out of your sight, keep them within your heart; for they are life to those who find them and health to a man's whole body.

Man 2: Above all else, guard your heart,
> for it is the wellspring of life.
>
> Put away perversity from your mouth;
> keep corrupt talk far from your lips.
>
> Let your eyes look straight ahead,
> fix your gaze directly before you.
>
> Make level paths for your feet
> and take only ways that are firm.
>
> Do not swerve to the right or the left;
> keep your foot from evil.

Man 1: My son, pay attention to my wisdom; lend your ear to my understanding.